Best Essential Air Fryer Cookbook 2021

Quick and Easy Guide to Air Fryer Recipes, Improve your Lifestyle Affordably and Stay Healthy!

Ricky Ward

Table of Contents

CONCLUSION 116

INTRODUCTION

An air fryer is a kitchen appliance designed to deliver a tasty, crispy, golden-brown morsel of food without the use of oil or other cooking fats. It uses hot air instead of oil or other cooking fats to cook food quickly and evenly.

The air fryer can be used for making fried chips in addition to other foods.

There are several varieties of air fryers. One of the main categories is made up of countertop air fryers designed for individual use in the kitchen. These models sit on the worktop or counter top and feature a basket that sits on a wire rack. This forms the base that holds hot air that cooks food as it passes through it.

air fryer's air fryers are designed to help you make healthy and filling meals. Our electric fryers are perfect for people who want fresh, homemade fries without all of the fat. Our air fryer features a light-weight aluminum design that lets you move the appliance from room to room without worry. Each air fryer is also equipped with a thermostat, making it easy to adjust the temperature as needed.

An air fryer is an appliance that cooks food using high-speed air circulation. It is a perfect alternative to deep frying, baking or roasting, and works great for cooking fast and healthy meals.

How Does an Air Fryer Work?

The fan draws warm air from the bottom of the chamber, which rises and cools as it circulates. The food is then placed in the middle of the basket, and the fan circulates air around it, cooking it all at once. Food cooks faster than if you fried it in oil or baked it in an oven. The food doesn't become soggy like fried food does, either. Because the air circulates around the food rather than through it, you can use much less oil in your Air Fryer. Best of all, since no oil is being used for cooking, there's much less of an environmental impact!

What Types of Air Fryers are Available?

Air fryers come in a variety of sizes as well as different colors and designs. You may find one that has a View Master-like chrome trim or one with a retro design pattern that blends easily into your décor. Some Air fryers are as small as a rice cooker while others can be used to make large batches of French fries with recipes you create on your tablet! Some Air Fryer models have "smart" features that allow you to cook multiple foods at the same time; others have timers so you can automatically set them for particular times during the day. All versions sterilize their own cooking plates by running them through a clean cycle between batches!

When you are looking for a new air fryer, you should take a look at air fryer Cookware. We have all of the features you are looking for in an air fryer, including built in racks that will allow you to cook a full size meal for your family. We also have a variety of accessories that will give you an even better cooking experience.

We are proud to introduce air fryer Cookware, the premier brand in air fryers. You can rest assured that we only use the best materials to ensure our products will work for years to come. Our air fryers feature built-in racks, so you can cook a full-size meal at once. They also include an adjustable thermostat that ranges from 120 to 500 degrees Fahrenheit.

Whether you are looking to impress your family with gourmet French fries or just want to make your favorite chicken drumsticks and vegetables, air fryer Cookware has everything you need. Every item has been carefully tested to ensure safe and responsible use. All of our products carry a One Year Limited Manufacturer Warranty, so you can be confident that they will serve your needs well.

Air fryer Italian Beef Stew

Preparation Time: 10 minutes
Cooking Time: 35 minutes
Servings: 6

Ingredients:

- 3 pounds of beef stew
- 1 onion, diced
- 4 carrots, diced
- 8-ounce baby portabella mushrooms, sliced
- 24-ounces of beef broth
- 15 ounce diced tomatoes, canned
- 3 tablespoons of white flour
- 1 teaspoon of dried basil leaves
- 1 teaspoon of dried thyme leaves
- 1 teaspoon of salt
- 1 teaspoon of pepper
- dried parsley

Directions:

1. Place meat in the air fryer.
2. Add in carrots, broth, flour, basil, thyme, salt, pepper, and tomatoes to air fryer and stir.
3. Close the lid.
4. Cook on high pressure for 35 minutes.
5. Quick release the pressure and carefully remove the lid.
6. Stir in the mushroom, stir the soup and then serve.

Nutrition: Calories – 385 Protein – 54 g. Fat – 12 g. Carbs – 12 g.

Air fryer Fish Stew

Preparation Time: 5 minutes
Cooking Time: 15 minutes
Servings: 4

Ingredients:

- 4 tablespoons of extra-virgin olive oil
- 1 medium red onion, chopped
- 4 garlic cloves, chopped
- ½ cup of dry white wine
- 8-ounce clam juice
- 2 1/2 cups of water
- ½ pound potatoes, diced
- 1 1/2 cups of fresh tomatoes with juices
- kosher salt
- black pepper for taste
- pinch of crushed red pepper for taste
- 2 pounds sea bass cut into 2-inch pieces
- 2 tablespoons lemon juice
- 2 tablespoons of fresh dill, chopped

Directions:

1. Use saute setting on your air fryer and cook onions in 2 tablespoons of olive oil for 3 minutes, until golden brown.
2. Add the chopped garlic, saute until fragrant.
3. Add the white wine, scrape up any brown bits, until about half of the wine has evaporated.
4. Add the clam juice, water, potatoes, tomatoes, salt, pepper, and a pinch of crushed red pepper.
5. Turn the saute off, cover and seal your air fryer, and set to manual high pressure for 5 minutes.
6. After this, quick release the pressure. Open the air fryer and turn the saute setting back on. Once the soup is simmering,

add the pieces of fish, and simmer for about 5 minutes, until the fish flakes apart easily.

7. Turn off saute mode, stir in lemon juice and fresh dill and remaining olive oil. Season to taste and serve.

Nutrition: Calories – 471 Protein – 43 g. Fat – 20 g. Carbs – 24 g.

Crushed Lentil Soup

Preparation Time: 10 minutes
Cooking Time: 30 minutes
Servings: 8

Ingredients:

- 2 tablespoons vegetable broth
- 1 onion, finely chopped
- 4 garlic cloves, minced
- 4 cups unsalted vegetable broth
- 2 cups of water
- 2 cups red split lentils
- 1 small pinch saffron
- 1 teaspoon coriander
- 1 teaspoon cumin
- ½ teaspoon freshly ground black pepper
- 1 teaspoon sea salt
- ½ teaspoon of red pepper flakes
- 2 bay leaves
- 2 tablespoons fresh lemon juice

Directions:

1. Put the air fryertosaute, add the vegetable broth, 2 tablespoons. Then put in the garlic and onions and cook until they are soft, about 4-5 minutes.
2. Add remaining ingredients except for bay leaves and lemon juice. Stir and then lock the lid of the air fryer.
3. Press cancel and choose the soup function. Set timer for 30 minutes. After the 30 minutes, let it sit for another 20 minutes to release the pressure.
4. Open the lid and add bay leaves and lemon juice, then stir for 5 minutes.
5. Remove bay leaves and serve.

Nutrition: Calories – 191 Protein – 11.8 g. Fat – 1.2 g. Carbs – 34.4 g.

Lemony Lentil Soup

Preparation Time: 10 minutes
Cooking Time: 25 minutes
Servings: 4

Ingredients:

- 1 tablespoon of olive oil
- 1 medium onion, peeled and diced
- 2 carrots, diced
- 5 garlic cloves, minced
- 6 cups of vegetable stock
- 1 1/2 cup of red lentils
- ⅔ cup of whole kernel corn
- 2 teaspoons of ground cumin
- 1 teaspoon of curry powder
- zest and juice of 1 lemon
- sea salt and black pepper to taste

Directions:

1. Choose the saute function on your air fryer and add oil. Add the onions and carrots and saute for 5 minutes. Stir occasionally until the onions are soft and translucent. Add garlic and saute for 1 more minute, until fragrant.
2. Pour in the vegetable stock, lentils, corn, cumin, and curry powder until combined
3. Make sure to lock the lid and set to "sealing."
4. Press and set for manual high pressure, and adjust the timer for 8 minutes. Cook, then carefully turn to venting for quick release. Once vented, remove the lid carefully.
5. Using a blender, puree the soup until it reaches your desired consistency.
6. Return the puree to the air fryer and stir in lemon zest and juice until combined.

7. Season with sea salt and black pepper to taste.
8. Serve warm.

Nutrition: Calories – 260 Protein – 16 g. Fat – 6 g. Carbs – 40 g.

Air fryer Vegetable Soup

Preparation Time: 10 minutes
Cooking Time: 20 minutes
Servings: 5

Ingredients:

- 2 tablespoons extra virgin olive oil
- ½ onion, chopped
- ½ green bell pepper, chopped
- 2 cloves garlic, minced
- 1 1/2 cups green cabbage, chopped
- 1 1/2 cups small cauliflower florets
- 1 cup chopped carrots
- ½ cup green beans, cut into small pieces
- 4 cups low-sodium vegetable broth
- 1 can diced tomatoes, no salt added
- 1 bay leaf
- ½ teaspoon salt
- 4 cups of chopped spinach
- 15 ounce cannellini beans, rinsed
- ¼ cup chopped basil

Directions:

1. Place olive oil in the air fryer and set to saute. Add onions, bell peppers, and garlic, then cook, stirring often until starting to soften, which will take 2-3 minutes.
2. Put in the carrots, cauliflower, cabbage, and green beans and cook for 4-5 minutes, stirring often.
3. Add the broth, tomatoes, bay leaf, and salt. Turn off the heat, lock the lid, and cook on high for 5 minutes.
4. Release the pressure using quick release, open the lid carefully, and remove bay leaf. Stir in the spinach, basil, and beans.

5. Ready to serve. May drizzle more olive oil on top if desired.

Nutrition: Calories – 192 Protein – 7.3 g. Fat – 6.6 g. Carbs – 26 g.

Air fryer Golden Lentil and Spinach Soup

Preparation Time: 10 minutes
Cooking Time: 25 minutes
Servings: 4

Ingredients:

- 2 teaspoons of olive oil
- ½ yellow onion, diced
- 2 carrots, peeled and diced
- 1 celery stock, diced
- 4 garlic cloves, minced
- 2 teaspoons ground cumin
- 1 teaspoon ground turmeric
- 1 teaspoon dried thyme
- 1 teaspoon kosher salt
- ¼ teaspoon freshly ground black pepper
- 1 cup dry brown lentils, rinsed well
- 4 cups low-sodium vegetable broth
- 8 ounces baby spinach

Directions:

1. Choose saute function of the air fryer and add oil. When hot, add onions, carrots, and celery. Saute, occasionally stirring, until tender, about 5 minutes.
2. Add garlic, cumin, turmeric, thyme, salt, and pepper. Cook and stir for one minute.
3. Stir in lentil and broth.
4. Place lid on air fryer and put the valve to "sealing." Press manual high pressure and set a timer for 12 minutes.
5. After 12 minutes, quick release pressure and then carefully remove the lid when done. Stir in the spinach, and add salt and pepper to taste.

Nutrition: Calories – 134 Protein – 9 g. Fat – 3 g. Carbs – 17 g.

SNACK

Soda Bread

Intermediate Recipe
Preparation Time: 15 minutes
Cooking Time: 30 minutes
Servings: 10

Ingredients:

- 3 cups whole-wheat flour
- 1 tablespoon sugar
- 2 teaspoon caraway seeds
- 1 teaspoon baking soda
- 1 teaspoon sea salt
- ¼ cup chilled butter, cubed into small pieces
- 1 large egg, beaten
- 1½ cups buttermilk

Directions:

1. In a large bowl, mix together the flour, sugar, caraway seeds, baking soda and salt and mix well.

2. With a pastry cutter, cut in the butter flour until coarse crumbs like mixture is formed.
3. Make a well in the center of flour mixture.
4. In the well, add the egg, followed by the buttermilk and with a spatula, mix until well combined.
5. With floured hand, shape the dough into a ball.
6. Place the dough onto a floured surface and lightly need it.
7. Shape the dough into a 6-inch ball.
8. With a serrated knife, score an X on the top of the dough.
9. Press "Power Button" of Air Fry Oven and turn the dial to select the "Air Crisp" mode.
10. Press the Time button and again turn the dial to set the cooking time to 30 minutes
11. Now push the Temp button and rotate the dial to set the temperature at 350 degrees F.
12. Press "Start/Pause" button to start.
13. When the unit beeps to show that it is preheated, open the lid.
14. Arrange the dough in lightly greased "Air Fry Basket" and insert in the oven.
15. Place the pan onto a wire rack to cool for about 10 minutes
16. Carefully, invert the bread onto wire rack to cool completely before slicing.
17. Cut the bread into desired-sized slices and serve.

Nutrition: Calories 205 Fat 5.9 g Carbs 31.8 g Protein 5.9 g

Baguette Bread

Intermediate Recipe

Preparation Time: 15 minutes

Cooking Time: 20 minutes

Servings: 8

Ingredients:

- ¾ cup warm water
- ¾ teaspoon quick yeast
- ½ teaspoon demerara sugar
- 1 cup bread flour
- ½ cup whole-wheat flour
- ½ cup oat flour
- 1¼ teaspoons salt

Directions:

1. In a large bowl, place the water and sprinkle with yeast and sugar.
2. Set aside for 5 minutes or until foamy.
3. Add the bread flour and salt mix until a stiff dough form.

4. Put the dough onto a floured surface and with your hands, knead until smooth and elastic.
5. Now, shape the dough into a ball.
6. Place the dough into a slightly oiled bowl and turn to coat well.
7. With a plastic wrap, cover the bowl and place in a warm place for about 1 hour or until doubled in size.
8. With your hands, punch down the dough and form into a long slender loaf.
9. Place the loaf onto a lightly greased baking sheet and set aside in warm place, uncovered, for about 30 minutes
10. Press "Power Button" of Air Fry Oven and turn the dial to select the "Air Bake" mode.
11. Press the Time button and again turn the dial to set the cooking time to 20 minutes
12. Now push the Temp button and rotate the dial to set the temperature at 450 degrees F.
13. Press "Start/Pause" button to start.
14. When the unit beeps to show that it is preheated, open the lid.
15. Carefully, arrange the dough onto the "Wire Rack" and insert in the oven.
16. Carefully, invert the bread onto wire rack to cool completely before slicing.
17. Cut the bread into desired-sized slices and serve.

Nutrition: Calories 114 Fat 0.8 g Carbs 22.8 g Protein 3.8 g

Yogurt Bread

Intermediate Recipe
Preparation Time: 20 minutes
Cooking Time: 40 minutes
Servings: 10

Ingredients:

- 1½ cups warm water, divided
- 1½ teaspoons active dry yeast
- 1 teaspoon sugar
- 3 cups all-purpose flour
- 1 cup plain Greek yogurt
- 2 teaspoons kosher salt

Directions:

1. Add ½ cup of the warm water, yeast and sugar in the bowl of a stand mixer, fitted with the dough hook attachment and mix well.
2. Set aside for about 5 minutes
3. Add the flour, yogurt, and salt and mix on medium-low speed until the dough comes together.
4. Then, mix on medium speed for 5 minutes
5. Place the dough into a bowl.
6. With a plastic wrap, cover the bowl and place in a warm place for about 2-3 hours or until doubled in size.

7. Transfer the dough onto a lightly floured surface and shape into a smooth ball.
8. Place the dough onto a greased parchment paper-lined rack.
9. With a kitchen towel, cover the dough and let rest for 15 minutes
10. With a very sharp knife, cut a 4x½-inch deep cut down the center of the dough.
11. Press "Power Button" of Air Fry Oven and turn the dial to select the "Air Roast" mode.
12. Press the Time button and again turn the dial to set the cooking time to 40 minutes
13. Now push the Temp button and rotate the dial to set the temperature at 325 degrees F.
14. Press "Start/Pause" button to start.
15. When the unit beeps to show that it is preheated, open the lid.
16. Carefully, arrange the dough onto the "Wire Rack" and insert in the oven.
17. Carefully, invert the bread onto wire rack to cool completely before slicing.
18. Cut the bread into desired-sized slices and serve.

Nutrition: Calories 157 Fat 0.7 g Carbs 31 g Protein 5.5 g

Sunflower Seed Bread

Intermediate Recipe

Preparation Time: 15 minutes

Cooking Time: 18 minutes

Servings: 6

Ingredients:

- 2/3 cup whole-wheat flour
- 2/3 cup plain flour
- 1/3 cup sunflower seeds
- ½ sachet instant yeast
- 1 teaspoon salt
- 2/3-1 cup lukewarm water

Directions:

1. In a bowl, mix together the flours, sunflower seeds, yeast, and salt.
2. Slowly, add in the water, stirring continuously until a soft dough ball form.
3. Now, move the dough onto a lightly floured surface and knead for about 5 minutes using your hands.
4. Make a ball from the dough and place into a bowl.

5. With a plastic wrap, cover the bowl and place at a warm place for about 30 minutes

6. Grease a cake pan.

7. Coat the top of dough with water and place into the prepared cake pan.

8. Press "Power Button" of Air Fry Oven and turn the dial to select the "Air Crisp" mode.

9. Press the Time button and again turn the dial to set the cooking time to 18 minutes

10. Now push the Temp button and rotate the dial to set the temperature at 390 degrees F.

11. Press "Start/Pause" button to start.

12. When the unit beeps to show that it is preheated, open the lid.

13. Arrange the pan in "Air Fry Basket" and insert in the oven.

14. Place the pan onto a wire rack to cool for about 10 minutes

15. Carefully, invert the bread onto wire rack to cool completely before slicing.

16. Cut the bread into desired-sized slices and serve.

Nutrition: Calories 132 Fat 1.7 g Carbs 24.4 g Protein 4.9 g

Date Bread

Intermediate Recipe

Preparation Time: 15 minutes

Cooking Time: 22 minutes

Servings: 10

Ingredients:

- 2½ cup dates, pitted and chopped
- ¼ cup butter
- 1 cup hot water
- 1½ cups flour
- ½ cup brown sugar
- 1 teaspoon baking powder
- 1 teaspoon baking soda
- ½ teaspoon salt
- 1 egg

Directions:

1. In a large bowl, add the dates, butter and top with the hot water.
2. Set aside for about 5 minutes
3. In another bowl, mix together the flour, brown sugar, baking powder, baking soda, and salt.

4. In the same bowl of dates, mix well the flour mixture, and egg.
5. Grease a baking pan.
6. Place the mixture into the prepared pan.
7. Press "Power Button" of Air Fry Oven and turn the dial to select the "Air Crisp" mode.
8. Press the Time button and again turn the dial to set the cooking time to 22 minutes
9. Now push the Temp button and rotate the dial to set the temperature at 340 degrees F.
10. Press "Start/Pause" button to start.
11. When the unit beeps to show that it is preheated, open the lid.
12. Arrange the pan in "Air Fry Basket" and insert in the oven.
13. Place the pan onto a wire rack to cool for about 10 minutes
14. Carefully, invert the bread onto wire rack to cool completely before slicing.
15. Cut the bread into desired-sized slices and serve.

Nutrition: Calories 269 Fat 5.4 g Carbs 55.1 g Protein 3.6 g

Date & Walnut Bread

thebellyrulesthemind.net

Intermediate Recipe
Preparation Time: 15 minutes
Cooking Time: 35 minutes
Servings: 5

Ingredients:

- 1 cup dates, pitted and sliced
- ¾ cup walnuts, chopped
- 1 tablespoon instant coffee powder
- 1 tablespoon hot water
- 1¼ cups plain flour
- ¼ teaspoon salt
- ½ teaspoon baking powder
- ½ teaspoon baking soda
- ½ cup condensed milk
- ½ cup butter, softened
- ½ teaspoon vanilla essence

Directions:

1. In a large bowl, add the dates, butter and top with the hot water.

2. Set aside for about 30 minutes

3. Dry out well and set aside.

4. In a small bowl, add the coffee powder and hot water and mix well.

5. In a large bowl, mix together the flour, baking powder, baking soda and salt.

6. In another large bowl, add the condensed milk and butter and beat until smooth.

7. Add the flour mixture, coffee mixture and vanilla essence and mix until well combined.

8. Fold in dates and ½ cup of walnut.

9. Line a baking pan with a lightly greased parchment paper.

10. Place the mixture into the prepared pan and sprinkle with the remaining walnuts.

11. Press "Power Button" of Air Fry Oven and turn the dial to select the "Air Crisp" mode.

12. Press the Time button and again turn the dial to set the cooking time to 35 minutes

13. Now push the Temp button and rotate the dial to set the temperature at 320 degrees F.

14. Press "Start/Pause" button to start.

15. When the unit beeps to show that it is preheated, open the lid.

16. Arrange the pan in "Air Fry Basket" and insert in the oven.

17. Place the pan onto a wire rack to cool for about 10 minutes

18. Carefully, invert the bread onto wire rack to cool completely before slicing.

19. Cut the bread into desired-sized slices and serve.

Nutrition: Calories 593 Fat 32.6 g Carbs 69.4 g Protein 11.2 g

Brown Sugar Banana Bread

Intermediate Recipe
Preparation Time: 15 minutes
Cooking Time: 30 minutes
Servings: 4

Ingredients:

- 1 egg
- 1 ripe banana, peeled and mashed
- ¼ cup milk
- 2 tablespoons canola oil
- 2 tablespoons brown sugar
- ¾ cup plain flour
- ½ teaspoon baking soda

Directions:

1. Line a very small baking pan with a greased parchment paper.
2. In a small bowl, add the egg and banana and beat well.
3. Add the milk, oil and sugar and beat until well combined.
4. Add the flour and baking soda and mix until just combined.
5. Place the mixture into prepared pan.

6. Press "Power Button" of Air Fry Oven and turn the dial to select the "Air Crisp" mode.
7. Press the Time button and again turn the dial to set the cooking time to 30 minutes
8. Now push the Temp button and rotate the dial to set the temperature at 320 degrees F.
9. Press "Start/Pause" button to start.
10. When the unit beeps to show that it is preheated, open the lid.
11. Arrange the pan in "Air Fry Basket" and insert in the oven.
12. Place the pan onto a wire rack to cool for about 10 minutes
13. Carefully, invert the bread onto wire rack to cool completely before slicing.
14. Cut the bread into desired-sized slices and serve.

Nutrition: Calories 214 Fat 8.7 g Carbs 29.9 g Protein 4.6 g

Cinnamon Banana Bread

Basic Recipe
Preparation Time: 15 minutes
Cooking Time: 20 minutes
Servings: 8

Ingredients:

- 1 1/3 cups flour
- 2/3 cup sugar
- 1 teaspoon baking soda
- 1 teaspoon baking powder
- 1 teaspoon ground cinnamon
- 1 teaspoon salt
- ½ cup milk
- ½ cup olive oil
- 3 bananas, peeled and sliced

Directions:

1. In the bowl of a stand mixer, add all the ingredients and mix well.
2. Grease a loaf pan.
3. Place the mixture into the prepared pan.

4. Press "Power Button" of Air Fry Oven and turn the dial to select the "Air Crisp" mode.
5. Press the Time button and again turn the dial to set the cooking time to 20 minutes
6. Now push the Temp button and rotate the dial to set the temperature at 330 degrees F.
7. Press "Start/Pause" button to start.
8. When the unit beeps to show that it is preheated, open the lid.
9. Arrange the pan in "Air Fry Basket" and insert in the oven.
10. Place the pan onto a wire rack to cool for about 10 minutes
11. Carefully, invert the bread onto wire rack to cool completely before slicing.
12. Cut the bread into desired-sized slices and serve.

Nutrition: Calories 295 Fat 13.3g Carbs 44 g Protein 3.1 g

Banana & Walnut Bread

Basic Recipe
Preparation Time: 15 minutes
Cooking Time: 25 minutes
Servings: 10

Ingredients:

- 1½ cups self-rising flour
- ¼ teaspoon bicarbonate of soda
- 5 tablespoons plus 1 teaspoon butter
- 2/3 cup plus ½ tablespoon caster sugar
- 2 medium eggs
- 3½ oz. walnuts, chopped
- 2 cups bananas, peeled and mashed

Directions:

1. In a bowl, mix together the flour and bicarbonate of soda.
2. In another bowl, add the butter, and sugar and beat until pale and fluffy.
3. Add the eggs, one at a time along with a little flour and mix well.
4. Stir in the remaining flour and walnuts.
5. Add the bananas and mix until well combined.
6. Grease a loaf pan.

7. Place the mixture into the prepared pan.
8. Press "Power Button" of Air Fry Oven and turn the dial to select the "Air Crisp" mode.
9. Press the Time button and again turn the dial to set the cooking time to 10 minutes
10. Now push the Temp button and rotate the dial to set the temperature at 355 degrees F.
11. Press "Start/Pause" button to start.
12. When the unit beeps to show that it is preheated, open the lid.
13. Arrange the pan in "Air Fry Basket" and insert in the oven.
14. After 10 minutes of cooking, set the temperature at 338 degrees F for 15 minutes
15. Place the pan onto a wire rack to cool for about 10 minutes
16. Carefully, invert the bread onto wire rack to cool completely before slicing.
17. Cut the bread into desired-sized slices and serve.

Nutrition: Calories 270 Fat 12.8 g Carbs 35.5 g Protein 5.8 g

Banana & Raisin Bread

Intermediate Recipe
Preparation Time: 15 minutes
Cooking Time: 40 minutes
Servings: 6

Ingredients:

- 1½ cups cake flour
- 1 teaspoon baking soda
- ½ teaspoon ground cinnamon
- Salt, to taste
- ½ cup vegetable oil
- 2 eggs
- ½ cup sugar
- ½ teaspoon vanilla extract
- 3 medium bananas, peeled and mashed
- ½ cup raisins, chopped finely

Directions:

1. In a large bowl, mix together the flour, baking soda, cinnamon, and salt.
2. In another bowl, beat well eggs and oil.
3. Add the sugar, vanilla extract, and bananas and beat until well combined.

4. Add the flour mixture and stir until just combined.
5. Place the mixture into a lightly greased baking pan and sprinkle with raisins.
6. With a piece of foil, cover the pan loosely.
7. Press "Power Button" of Air Fry Oven and turn the dial to select the "Air Bake" mode.
8. Press the Time button and again turn the dial to set the cooking time to 30 minutes
9. Now push the Temp button and rotate the dial to set the temperature at 300 degrees F.
10. Press "Start/Pause" button to start.
11. When the unit beeps to show that it is preheated, open the lid.
12. Arrange the pan in "Air Fry Basket" and insert in the oven.
13. After 30 minutes of cooking, set the temperature to 285 degrees F for 10 minutes
14. Place the pan onto a wire rack to cool for about 10 minutes
15. Carefully, invert the bread onto wire rack to cool completely before slicing.
16. Cut the bread into desired-sized slices and serve.

Nutrition: Calories 448 Fat 20.2 g Carbs 63.9 g Protein 6.1 g

3-Ingredients Banana Bread

Basic Recipe
Preparation Time: 10 minutes
Cooking Time: 20 minutes
Servings: 6

Ingredients:

- 2 (6.4-oz.) banana muffin mix
- 1 cup water
- 1 ripe banana, peeled and mashed

Directions:

1. In a bowl, add all the ingredients and with a whisk, mix until well combined.
2. Place the mixture into a lightly greased loaf pan.
3. Press "Power Button" of Air Fry Oven and turn the dial to select the "Air Bake" mode.
4. Press the Time button and again turn the dial to set the cooking time to 20 minutes
5. Now push the Temp button and rotate the dial to set the temperature at 360 degrees F.

6. Press "Start/Pause" button to start.
7. When the unit beeps to show that it is preheated, open the lid.
8. Arrange the pan in "Air Fry Basket" and insert in the oven.
9. Place the pan onto a wire rack to cool for about 10 minutes
10. Carefully, invert the bread onto wire rack to cool completely before slicing.
11. Cut the bread into desired-sized slices and serve.

Nutrition: Calories 144 Fat 3.8 g Carbs 25.5 g Protein 1.9 g

Yogurt Banana Bread

Intermediate Recipe

Preparation Time: 15 minutes

Cooking Time: 28 minutes

Servings: 5

Ingredients:

- 1 medium very ripe banana, peeled and mashed
- 1 large egg
- 1 tablespoon canola oil
- 1 tablespoon plain Greek yogurt
- ¼ teaspoon pure vanilla extract
- ½ cup all-purpose flour
- ¼ cup granulated white sugar
- ¼ teaspoon ground cinnamon
- ¼ teaspoon baking soda
- 1/8 teaspoon sea salt

Directions:

1. In a bowl, add the mashed banana, egg, oil, yogurt and vanilla and beat until well combined.
2. Add the flour, sugar, baking soda, cinnamon and salt and mix until just combined.
3. Place the mixture into a lightly greased mini loaf pan.

---

4. Press "Power Button" of Air Fry Oven and turn the dial to select the "Air Bake" mode.
5. Press the Time button and again turn the dial to set the cooking time to 28 minutes
6. Now push the Temp button and rotate the dial to set the temperature at 350 degrees F.
7. Press "Start/Pause" button to start.
8. When the unit beeps to show that it is preheated, open the lid.
9. Arrange the pan in "Air Fry Basket" and insert in the oven.
10. Place the pan onto a wire rack to cool for about 10 minutes
11. Carefully, invert the bread onto wire rack to cool completely before slicing.
12. Cut the bread into desired-sized slices and serve.

Nutrition: Calories 145 Fat 4 g Carbs 25 g Protein 3 g

Sour Cream Banana Bread

Intermediate Recipe
Preparation Time: 15 minutes
Cooking Time: 37 minutes
Servings: 8

Ingredients:

- ¾ cup all-purpose flour
- ¼ teaspoon baking soda
- ¼ teaspoon salt
- 2 ripe bananas, peeled and mashed
- ½ cup granulated sugar
- ¼ cup sour cream
- ¼ cup vegetable oil
- 1 large egg
- ½ teaspoon pure vanilla extract

Directions:

1. In a large bowl, mix together the flour, baking soda and salt.

2. In another bowl, add the bananas, egg, sugar, sour cream, oil and vanilla and beat until well combined.
3. Add the flour mixture and mix until just combined.
4. Place the mixture into a lightly greased pan. Press "Power Button" of Air Fry Oven and turn the dial to select the "Air Crisp" mode.
5. Press the Time button and again turn the dial to set the cooking time to 37 minutes
6. Now push the Temp button and rotate the dial to set the temperature at 310 degrees F. Press "Start/Pause" button to start.
7. When the unit beeps to show that it is preheated, open the lid. Arrange the pan in "Air Fry Basket" and insert in the oven.
8. Place the pan onto a wire rack to cool for about 10 minutes
9. Carefully, invert the bread onto wire rack to cool completely before slicing.
10. Cut the bread into desired-sized slices and serve.

Nutrition: Calories 201 Fat 9.2g Carbs 28.6g Protein 2.6g

Peanut Butter Banana Bread

Intermediate Recipe
Preparation Time: 15 minutes
Cooking Time: 40 minutes
Servings: 6

Ingredients:

- 1 cup plus 1 tablespoon all-purpose flour
- ¼ teaspoon baking soda
- 1 teaspoon baking powder
- ¼ teaspoon salt
- 1 large egg
- 1/3 cup granulated sugar
- ¼ cup canola oil
- 2 tablespoons creamy peanut butter
- 2 tablespoons sour cream

- 1 teaspoon vanilla extract
- 2 medium ripe bananas, peeled and mashed
- ¾ cup walnuts, roughly chopped

Directions:

1. In a bowl and mix the flour, baking powder, baking soda, and salt together.
2. In another large bowl, add the egg, sugar, oil, peanut butter, sour cream, and vanilla extract and beat until well combined.
3. Add the bananas and beat until well combined.
4. Add the flour mixture and mix until just combined.
5. Gently, fold in the walnuts.
6. Place the mixture into a lightly greased pan.
7. Press "Power Button" of Air Fry Oven and turn the dial to select the "Air Crisp" mode.
8. Press the Time button and again turn the dial to set the cooking time to 40 minutes
9. Now push the Temp button and rotate the dial to set the temperature at 330 degrees F.
10. Press "Start/Pause" button to start.
11. When the unit beeps to show that it is preheated, open the lid.
12. Arrange the pan in "Air Fry Basket" and insert in the oven.
13. Place the pan onto a wire rack to cool for about 10 minutes
14. Carefully, invert the bread onto wire rack to cool completely before slicing.
15. Cut the bread into desired-sized slices and serve.

Nutrition: Calories 384 Fat 23 g Carbs 39.3 g Protein 8.9 g

Chocolate Banana Bread

Basic Recipe
Preparation Time: 15 minutes
Cooking Time: 20 minutes
Servings: 8
Ingredients:

- 2 cups flour
- ½ teaspoon baking soda
- ½ teaspoon baking powder
- ½ teaspoon salt
- ¾ cup sugar
- 1/3 cup butter, softened
- 3 eggs
- 1 tablespoon vanilla extract
- 1 cup milk
- ½ cup bananas, peeled and mashed
- 1 cup chocolate chips

Directions:

1. In a bowl, mix together the flour, baking soda, baking powder, and salt.
2. In another large bowl, add the butter, and sugar and beat until light and fluffy.
3. Add the eggs, and vanilla extract and whisk until well combined.
4. Add the flour mixture and mix until well combined.
5. Add the milk, and mashed bananas and mix well.
6. Gently, fold in the chocolate chips. Place the mixture into a lightly greased loaf pan.
7. Press "Power Button" of Air Fry Oven and turn the dial to select the "Air Crisp" mode.
8. Press the Time button and again turn the dial to set the cooking time to 20 minutes
9. Now push the Temp button and rotate the dial to set the temperature at 360 degrees F.
10. Press "Start/Pause" button to start.When the unit beeps to show that it is preheated, open the lid.
11. Arrange the pan in "Air Fry Basket" and insert in the oven.
12. Place the pan onto a wire rack to cool for about 10 minutesCarefully, invert the bread onto wire rack to cool completely before slicing.
13. Cut the bread into desired-sized slices and serve.

Nutrition: Calories 416 Fat 16.5 g Carbs 59.2 g Protein 8.1 g

Allspice Chicken Wings

Basic Recipe
Preparation Time:
Cooking Time: 45 minutes
Serving: 8

Ingredients:

- ½ tsp celery salt
- ½ tsp bay leaf powder
- ½ tsp ground black pepper
- ½ tsp paprika
- ¼ tsp dry mustard
- ¼ tsp cayenne pepper
- ¼ tsp allspice
- 2 pounds chicken wings

Directions:

1. Grease the air fryer basket and preheat to 340 F. In a bowl, mix celery salt, bay leaf powder, black pepper, paprika, dry mustard, cayenne pepper, and allspice. Coat the wings thoroughly in this mixture.
2. Arrange the wings in an even layer in the basket of the air fryer. Cook the chicken until it's no longer pink around the bone, for 30 minutes then, increase the temperature to 380 F and cook for 6 minutes more, until crispy on the outside.

Nutrition:
Calories 332 Fat 10.1 g Carbs 31.3 g Protein 12 g

Friday Night Pineapple Sticky Ribs

Basic Recipe

Preparation Time: 10 minutes

Cooking Time: 20 minutes

Servings: 4

Ingredients:

- 2 lb. cut spareribs
- 7 oz salad dressing
- 1 (5-oz) can pineapple juice
- 2 cups water
- Garlic salt to taste
- Salt and black pepper

Directions:

1. Sprinkle the ribs with salt and pepper, and place them in a saucepan. Pour water and cook the ribs for 12 minutes on high heat.
2. Dry out the ribs and arrange them in the fryer; sprinkle with garlic salt. Cook it for 15minutes at 390 F.
3. Prepare the sauce by combining the salad dressing and the pineapple juice. Serve the ribs drizzled with the sauce.

Nutrition: Calories 316 Fat 3.1 g Carbs 1.9 g Protein 5 g

Egg Roll Wrapped with Cabbage and Prawns

Intermediate Recipe
Preparation Time: 10 minutes
Cooking Time: 40 minutes
Servings: 4

Ingredients:

- 2 tbsp vegetable oil
- 1-inch piece fresh ginger, grated
- 1 tbsp minced garlic
- 1 carrot, cut into strips
- ¼ cup chicken broth
- 2 tbsp reduced-sodium soy sauce
- 1 tbsp sugar
- 1 cup shredded Napa cabbage
- 1 tbsp sesame oil
- 8 cooked prawns, minced
- 1 egg
- 8 egg roll wrappers

Directions:

1. In a skillet over high heat, heat vegetable oil, and cook ginger and garlic for 40 seconds, until fragrant. Stir in carrot

and cook for another 2 minutes Pour in chicken broth, soy sauce, and sugar and bring to a boil.

2. Add cabbage and let simmer until softened, for 4 minutes Remove skillet from the heat and stir in sesame oil. Let cool for 15 minutes Strain cabbage mixture, and fold in minced prawns. Whisk an egg in a small bowl. Fill each egg roll wrapper with prawn mixture, arranging the mixture just below the center of the wrapper.

3. Fold the bottom part over the filling and tuck under. Fold in both sides and tightly roll up. Use the whisked egg to seal the wrapper. Repeat until all egg rolls are ready. Place the rolls into a greased air fryer basket, spray them with oil and cook for 12 minutes at 370 F, turning once halfway through.

Nutrition: Calories 215 Fat 7.9 g Carbs 6.7 g Protein 8 g

Sesame Garlic Chicken Wings

Intermediate Recipe

Preparation Time: 10 minutes

Cooking Time: 40 minutes

Servings: 4

Ingredients:

- 1-pound chicken wings
- 1 cup soy sauce, divided
- ½ cup brown sugar
- ½ cup apple cider vinegar
- 2 tbsp fresh ginger, minced
- 2 tbsp fresh garlic, minced
- 1 tsp finely ground black pepper
- 2 tbsp cornstarch
- 2 tbsp cold water
- 1 tsp sesame seeds

Directions:

1. In a bowl, add chicken wings, and pour in half cup soy sauce. Refrigerate for 20 minutes; Dry out and pat dry. Arrange the wings in the air fryer and cook for 30 minutes

at 380 F, turning once halfway through. Make sure you check them towards the end to avoid overcooking.

2. In a skillet and over medium heat, stir sugar, half cup soy sauce, vinegar, ginger, garlic, and black pepper. Cook until sauce has reduced slightly, about 4 to 6 minutes

3. Dissolve 2 tbsp of cornstarch in cold water, in a bowl, and stir in the slurry into the sauce, until it thickens, for 2 minutes Pour the sauce over wings and sprinkle with sesame seeds.

Nutrition: Calories 413 Fat 8.3 g Carbs 7 g Protein 8.3 g

Savory Chicken Nuggets with Parmesan Cheese

Basic Recipe

Preparation Time: 5 minutes

Cooking Time: 20 minutes

Servings: 4

Ingredients:

- 1 lb. chicken breast, boneless, skinless, cubed
- ½ tsp ground black pepper
- ¼ tsp kosher salt
- ¼ tsp seasoned salt
- 2 tbsp olive oil
- 5 tbsp plain breadcrumbs
- 2 tbsp panko breadcrumbs
- 2 tbsp grated Parmesan cheese

Directions:

1. Preheat the air fryer to 380 F and grease. Season the chicken with pepper, kosher salt, and seasoned salt; set aside. In a bowl, pour olive oil. In a separate bowl, add crumb, and Parmesan cheese.

2. Place the chicken pieces in the oil to coat, then dip into breadcrumb mixture, and transfer to the air fryer. Work in batches if needed. Lightly spray chicken with cooking spray.
3. Cook the chicken for 10 minutes, flipping once halfway through. Cook until golden brown on the outside and no more pink on the inside.

Nutrition: Calories 312 Fat 8.9 g Carbs 7 g Protein 10 g

Butternut Squash with Thyme

Basic Recipe
Preparation Time: 5 minutes
Cooking Time: 20 minutes
Servings: 4

Ingredients:

- 2 cups peeled, butternut squash, cubed
- 1 tbsp olive oil
- ¼ tsp salt
- ¼ tsp black pepper
- ¼ tsp dried thyme
- 1 tbsp finely chopped fresh parsley

Directions:

1. In a bowl, add squash, oil, salt, pepper, and thyme, and toss until squash is well-coated.
2. Place squash in the air fryer and cook for 14 minutes at 360 F.
3. When ready, sprinkle with freshly chopped parsley and serve chilled.

Nutrition: Calories 219 Fat 4.3 g Carbs 9.4 g Protein 7.8 g

Chicken Breasts in Golden Crumb

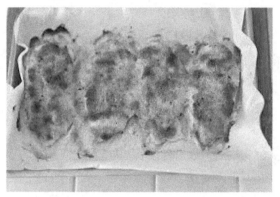

Basic Recipe

Preparation Time: 10 minutes

Cooking Time: 25 minutes

Servings: 4

Ingredients:

- 1 ½ lb. chicken breasts, boneless, cut into strips
- 1 egg, lightly beaten
- 1 cup seasoned breadcrumbs
- Salt and black pepper to taste
- ½ tsp dried oregano

Directions:

1. Preheat the air fryer to 390 F. Season the chicken with oregano, salt, and black pepper. In a small bowl, whisk in some salt and pepper to the beaten egg. In a separate bowl, add the crumbs. Dip chicken tenders in the egg wash, then in the crumbs.
2. Roll the strips in the breadcrumbs and press firmly, so the breadcrumbs stick well. Spray the chicken tenders with cooking spray and arrange them in the air fryer. Cook for 14 minutes, until no longer pink in the center, and nice and crispy on the outside.

Nutrition: Calories 223 Fat 3.2 g Carbs 4.3 g Protein 5 g

Yogurt Chicken Tacos

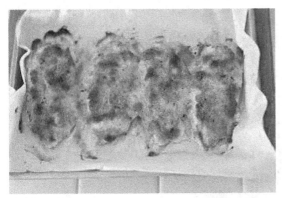

Basic Recipe

Preparation Time: 5 minutes

Cooking Time: 20 minutes

Servings: 4

Ingredients:

- 1 cup cooked chicken, shredded
- 1 cup shredded mozzarella cheese
- ¼ cup salsa
- ¼ cup Greek yogurt
- Salt and ground black pepper
- 8 flour tortillas

Directions:

1. In a bowl, mix chicken, cheese, salsa, and yogurt, and season with salt and pepper. Spray one side of the tortilla with cooking spray. Lay 2 tbsp of the chicken mixture at the center of the non-oiled side of each tortilla.
2. Roll tightly around the mixture. Arrange taquitos into your air fryer basket, without overcrowding. Cook in batches if needed. Place the seam side down, or it will unravel during cooking crisps.
3. Cook it for 12 to 14 minutes, or until crispy, at 380 F.

Nutrition: Calories 312 Fat 3 g Carbs 6.5 g Protein 6.2 g

—

Flawless Kale Chips

Basic Recipe

Preparation Time: 5 minutes

Cooking Time: 20 minutes

Servings: 4

Ingredients:

- 4 cups chopped kale leaves; stems removed
- 2 tbsp olive oil
- 1 tsp garlic powder
- ½ tsp salt
- ¼ tsp onion powder
- ¼ tsp black pepper

Directions:

1. In a bowl, mix kale and oil together, until well-coated. Add in garlic, salt, onion, and pepper and toss until well-coated. Arrange half the kale leaves to air fryer, in a single layer.
2. Cook for 8 minutes at 350 F, shaking once halfway through. Remove chips to a sheet to cool; do not touch.

Nutrition: Calories 312 Fat 5.3 g Carbs 5 g Protein 7 g

Cheese Fish Balls

Basic Recipe
Preparation Time: 5 minutes
Cooking Time: 40 minutes
Servings: 6
Ingredients:

- 1 cup smoked fish, flaked
- 2 cups cooked rice
- 2 eggs, lightly beaten
- 1 cup grated Grana Padano cheese
- ¼ cup finely chopped thyme
- Salt and black pepper to taste
- 1 cup panko crumbs

Directions:

1. In a bowl, add fish, rice, eggs, Parmesan cheese, thyme, salt and pepper into a bowl; stir to combine. Shape the mixture into 12 even-sized balls. Roll the balls in the crumbs then spray with oil.
2. Arrange the balls into the fryer and cook for 16 minutes at 400 F, until crispy.

Nutrition: Calories 234 Fat 5.2 g Carbs 4.3 g Protein 6.2 g

Vermicelli Noodles & Vegetables Rolls

Basic Recipe
Preparation Time: 5 minutes
Cooking Time: 25 minutes
Servings: 8

Ingredients:

- 8 spring roll wrappers
- 1 cup cooked and cooled vermicelli noodles
- 2 garlic cloves, finely chopped
- 1 tbsp minced fresh ginger
- 2 tbsp soy sauce
- 1 tsp sesame oil
- 1 red bell pepper, seeds removed, chopped
- 1 cup finely chopped mushrooms
- 1 cup finely chopped carrot
- ½ cup finely chopped scallions

Directions:

1. In a saucepan, add garlic, ginger, soy sauce, pepper, mushroom, carrot and scallions, and stir-fry over high heat

---

for a few minutes, until soft. Add in vermicelli noodles; remove from the heat.

2. Place the spring roll wrappers onto a working board. Spoon the dollops of veggie and noodle mixture at the center of each spring roll wrapper. Roll the spring rolls and tuck the corners and edges in to create neat and secure rolls.

3. Spray with oil and transfer them to the air fryer. Cook for 12 minutes at 340 F, turning once halfway through. Cook until golden and crispy. Serve with soy or sweet chili sauce.

Nutrition: Calories 312 Fat 5 g Carbs 5.4g Protein 3 g

Beef Balls with Mixed Herbs

Basic Recipe

Preparation Time: 5 minutes

Cooking Time: 25 minutes

Servings: 4

Ingredients:

- 1 lb. ground beef
- 1 onion, finely chopped
- 3 garlic cloves, finely chopped
- 2 eggs
- 1 cup breadcrumbs
- ½ cup fresh mixed herbs
- 1tbsp mustard
- Salt and black pepper to taste
- Olive oil

Directions:

1. In a bowl, add beef, onion, garlic, eggs, crumbs, herbs, mustard, salt, and pepper and mix with hands to combine.
2. Shape into balls and arrange them in the air fryer's basket. Drizzle with oil and cook for 16 minutes at 380 F, turning once halfway through.

Nutrition: Calories 315 Fat 5 g Carbs 9 g Protein 8 g

Roasted Pumpkin Seeds

Basic Recipe
Preparation Time: 10 minutes
Cooking Time: 40 minutes
Servings: 4

Ingredients:

- 1 cup pumpkin seeds, pulp removed, rinsed
- 1 tbsp butter, melted
- 1 tbsp brown sugar
- 1 tsp orange zest
- ½ tsp cardamom
- ½ tsp salt

Directions:

1. Cook the seeds for 4 minutes at 320 F, in your air fryer, to avoid moisture. In a bowl, whisk melted butter, sugar, zest, cardamom and salt.
2. Add the seeds to the bowl and toss to coat thoroughly.
3. Transfer the seeds to the air fryer and cook for 35 minutes at 300 F, shaking the basket every 10-12 minutes Cook until lightly browned.

Nutrition: Calories 536 Fat 42.86g Calcium: 71g Sodium: 571gp

Buttery Parmesan Broccoli Florets

Basic Recipe

Preparation Time: 5 minutes

Cooking Time: 20 minutes

Servings: 2

Ingredients:

- 2 tbsp butter, melted
- 1 egg white
- 1 garlic clove, grated
- ¼ tsp salt
- A pinch of black pepper
- ½ lb. broccoli florets
- ⅓ cup grated Parmesan cheese

Directions:

1. In a bowl, whisk together the butter, egg, garlic, salt, and black pepper.
2. Toss in broccoli to coat well.
3. Top with Parmesan cheese and; toss to coat.

4. Arrange broccoli in a single layer in the air fryer, without overcrowding.
5. Cook it in batches for 10 minutes at 360 F.
6. Remove to a serving plate and sprinkle with Parmesan cheese.

Nutrition: Calories 350 Fat 27 g Carbs 20g Protein 15 g

Spicy Chickpeas

Basic Recipe
Preparation Time: 5 minutes
Cooking Time: 10 minutes
Servings: 4

Ingredients:

- 1 (15-oz.) can chickpeas rinsed and Dry-out
- 1 tablespoon olive oil
- ½ teaspoon ground cumin
- ½ teaspoon cayenne pepper
- ½ teaspoon smoked paprika
- Salt, as required

Directions:

1. In a bowl, add all the ingredients and toss to coat well.
2. Press "Power Button" of Air Fry Oven and turn the dial to select the "Air Fry" mode.
3. Press the Time button and again turn the dial to set the cooking time to 10 minutes
4. Now push the Temp button and rotate the dial to set the temperature at 390 degrees F.
5. Press "Start/Pause" button to start.
6. When the unit beeps to show that it is preheated, open the lid.

---

7. Arrange the chickpeas in "Air Fry Basket" and insert in the oven.
8. Serve warm.

Nutrition: Calories 146 Fat 4.5 g Carbs 18.8 g Protein 6.3 g

Roasted Peanuts

Basic Recipe
Preparation Time: 5 minutes
Cooking Time: 14 minutes
Servings: 6

Ingredients:

- 1½ cups raw peanuts
- Nonstick cooking spray

Directions:

1. Press "Power Button" of Air Fry Oven and turn the dial to select the "Air Fry" mode. Press the Time button and again turn the dial to set the cooking time to 14 minutes

2. Now push the Temp button and rotate the dial to set the temperature at 320 degrees F. Press "Start/Pause" button to start.

3. When the unit beeps to show that it is preheated, open the lid.
4. Arrange the peanuts in "Air Fry Basket" and insert in the oven.
5. Toss the peanuts twice.
6. After 9 minutes of cooking, spray the peanuts with cooking spray.
7. Serve warm.

Nutrition: Calories 207 Fat 18 g Carbs 5.9 g Protein 9.4 g

Roasted Cashews

Basic Recipe
Preparation Time: 5 minutes
Cooking Time: 5 minutes
Servings: 6

Ingredients:

- 1½ cups raw cashew nuts
- 1 teaspoon butter, melted
- Salt and freshly ground black pepper, as needed

Directions:

1. In a bowl, mix together all the ingredients.
2. Press "Power Button" of Air Fry Oven and turn the dial to select the "Air Fry" mode.
3. Press the Time button and again turn the dial to set the cooking time to 5 minutes
4. Now push the Temp button and rotate the dial to set the temperature at 355 degrees F.
5. Press "Start/Pause" button to start.
6. When the unit beeps to show that it is preheated, open the lid.
7. Arrange the cashews in "Air Fry Basket" and insert in the oven.
8. Shake the cashews once halfway through.

Nutrition: Calories 202 Fat 16.5 g Carbs 11.2 g Protein 5.3 g

French Fries

Basic Recipe
Preparation Time: 15 minutes
Cooking Time: 30 minutes
Servings: 4

Ingredients:

- 1 lb. potatoes, peeled and cut into strips
- 3 tablespoons olive oil
- ½ teaspoon onion powder
- ½ teaspoon garlic powder
- 1 teaspoon paprika

Directions:

1. In a large bowl of water, soak the potato strips for about 1 hour.
2. Dry out the potato strips well and pat them dry with the paper towels.
3. In a large bowl, add the potato strips and the remaining ingredients and toss to coat well.

4. Press "Power Button" of Air Fry Oven and turn the dial to select the "Air Fry" mode.
5. Press the Time button and again turn the dial to set the cooking time to 30 minutes
6. Now push the Temp button and rotate the dial to set the temperature at 375 degrees F.
7. Press "Start/Pause" button to start.
8. When the unit beeps to show that it is preheated, open the lid.
9. Arrange the potato fries in "Air Fry Basket" and insert in the oven.
10. Serve warm.

Nutrition: Calories 172 Fat 10.7 g Carbs 18.6 g Protein 2.1 g

Zucchini Fries

Basic Recipe
Preparation Time: 10 minutes
Cooking Time: 20 minutes
Servings: 4

Ingredients:

- 1 lb. zucchini, sliced into 2½-inch sticks
- Salt, as required
- 2 tablespoons olive oil
- ¾ cup panko breadcrumbs

Directions:

1. In a colander, add the zucchini and sprinkle with salt. Set aside for about 10 minutes. Gently pat dry the zucchini sticks with the paper towels and coat with oil.
2. In a shallow dish, add the breadcrumbs.Coat the zucchini sticks with breadcrumbs evenly.
3. Press "Power Button" of Air Fry Oven and turn the dial to select the "Air Fry" mode.
4. Press the Time button and again turn the dial to set the cooking time to 12 minutes
5. Now push the Temp button and rotate the dial to set the temperature at 400 degrees F.
6. Press "Start/Pause" button to start.

7. When the unit beeps to show that it is preheated, open the lid.
8. Arrange the zucchini fries in "Air Fry Basket" and insert in the oven.
9. Serve warm.

Nutrition: Calories 151 Fat 8.6 g Carbs 6.9 g Protein 1.9 g

Spicy Carrot Fries

Basic Recipe
Preparation Time: 10 minutes
Cooking Time: 12 minutes
Servings: 2

Ingredients:

- 1 large carrot, peeled and cut into sticks
- 1 tablespoon fresh rosemary, chopped finely
- 1 tablespoon olive oil
- ¼ teaspoon cayenne pepper
- Salt and ground black pepper, as required

Directions:

1. In a bowl, add all the ingredients and mix well. Press "Power Button" of Air Fry Oven and turn the dial to select the "Air Fry" mode.
2. Press the Time button and again turn the dial to set the cooking time to 12 minutes
3. Now push the Temp button and rotate the dial to set the temperature at 390 degrees F.
4. Press "Start/Pause" button to start.

5. When the unit beeps to show that it is preheated, open the lid.
6. Arrange the carrot fries in "Air Fry Basket" and insert in the oven.
7. Serve warm.

Nutrition: Calories 81 Fat 8.3 g Carbs 4.7 g Protein 0.4 g

Cinnamon Carrot Fries

Basic Recipe
Preparation Time: 10 minutes
Cooking Time: 12 minutes
Servings: 6

Ingredients:

- 1 lb. carrots, peeled and cut into sticks
- 1 teaspoon maple syrup
- 1 teaspoon olive oil
- ½ teaspoon ground cinnamon
- Salt, to taste

Directions:

1. In a bowl, add all the ingredients and mix well.
2. Press "Power Button" of Air Fry Oven and turn the dial to select the "Air Fry" mode. Press the Time button and again turn the dial to set the cooking time to 12 minutes
3. Now push the Temp button and rotate the dial to set the temperature at 400 degrees F.
4. Press "Start/Pause" button to start.
5. When the unit beeps to show that it is preheated, open the lid.
6. Arrange the carrot fries in "Air Fry Basket" and insert in the oven.
7. Serve warm.

Nutrition: Calories 41 Fat 0.8 g Carbs 8.3 g Protein 0.6 g

Squash Fries

Basic Recipe
Preparation Time: 10 minutes
Cooking Time: 35 minutes
Servings: 2

Ingredients:

- 14 oz. butternut squash, peeled, seeded and cut into strips
- 2 teaspoons olive oil
- ½ teaspoon ground cinnamon
- ½ teaspoon red chili powder
- ¼ teaspoon garlic salt
- Salt and freshly ground black pepper, as needed

Directions:

1. In a bowl, add all the ingredients and toss to coat well. Press "Power Button" of Air Fry Oven and turn the dial to select the "Air Fry" mode.
2. Press the Time button and again turn the dial to set the cooking time to 30 minutes. Now push the Temp button and rotate the dial to set the temperature at 400 degrees F.

3. Press "Start/Pause" button to start. When the unit beeps to show that it is preheated, open the lid.
4. Arrange the squash fries in "Air Fry Basket" and insert in the oven.
5. Serve warm.

Nutrition: Calories 134 Fat 5 g Carbs 24.3 g Protein 2.1 g

Avocado Fries

Basic Recipe
Preparation Time: 15 minutes
Cooking Time: 7 minutes
Servings: 2

Ingredients:

- ¼ cup all-purpose flour
- Salt and freshly ground black pepper, as needed
- 1 egg 1 teaspoon water
- ½ cup panko breadcrumbs
- 1 avocado, peeled, pitted and sliced into 8 pieces
- Non-stick cooking spray

Directions:

1. In a shallow bowl, mix together the flour, salt, and black pepper.
2. In a second bowl, mix well egg and water.
3. In a third bowl, put the breadcrumbs.
4. Coat the avocado slices with flour mixture, then dip into egg mixture and finally, coat evenly with the breadcrumbs.

5. Now, spray the avocado slices evenly with cooking spray.
6. Press "Power Button" of Air Fry Oven and turn the dial to select the "Air Fry" mode.
7. Press the Time button and again turn the dial to set the cooking time to 7 minutes
8. Now push the Temp button and rotate the dial to set the temperature at 400 degrees F.
9. Press "Start/Pause" button to start.
10. When the unit beeps to show that it is preheated, open the lid.
11. Arrange the avocado fries in "Air Fry Basket" and insert in the oven.
12. Serve warm.

Nutrition: Calories 340 Fat 14 g Carbs 30 g Protein 23 g

Dill Pickle Fries

Basic Recipe
Preparation Time: 15 minutes
Cooking Time: 15 minutes
Servings: 8

Ingredients:

- 1 (16-oz.) jar spicy dill pickle spears Dry out and pat dried
- ¾ cup all-purpose flour
- ½ teaspoon paprika
- 1 egg, beaten
- ¼ cup milk
- 1 cup panko breadcrumbs
- Nonstick cooking spray

Directions:

1. In a shallow dish, mix together the flour, and paprika.
2. In a second dish, place the milk and egg and mix well.
3. In a third dish, put the breadcrumbs.
4. Coat the pickle spears with flour mixture, then dip into egg mixture and finally, coat evenly with the breadcrumbs.
5. Now, spray the pickle spears evenly with cooking spray.
6. Press "Power Button" of Air Fry Oven and turn the dial to select the "Air Fry" mode.

7. Press the Time button and again turn the dial to set the cooking time to 15 minutes

8. Now push the Temp button and rotate the dial to set the temperature at 400 degrees F.

9. Press "Start/Pause" button to start. When the unit beeps to show that it is preheated, open the lid.

10. Arrange the squash fries in "Air Fry Basket" and insert in the oven.

11. Serve warm.

12. Flip the fries once halfway through.

13. Serve warm.

Nutrition: Calories 110 Fat 1.9 g Carbs 12.8 g Protein 2.7 g

Mozzarella Sticks

Basic Recipe
Preparation Time: 15 minutes
Cooking Time: 12 minutes
Servings: 3

Ingredients:

- ¼ cup white flour
- 2 eggs
- 3 tablespoons nonfat milk
- 1 cup plain breadcrumbs
- 1 lb. Mozzarella cheese block cut into 3x½-inch sticks

Directions:

1. In a shallow dish, add the flour.
2. In a second shallow dish, mix together the eggs, and milk.
3. In a third shallow dish, place the breadcrumbs.
4. Coat the Mozzarella sticks with flour, then dip into egg mixture and finally, coat evenly with the breadcrumbs.
5. Press "Power Button" of Air Fry Oven and turn the dial to select the "Air Fry" mode.
6. Press the Time button and again turn the dial to set the cooking time to 12 minutes

---

7. Now push the Temp button and rotate the dial to set the temperature at 400 degrees F.
8. Press "Start/Pause" button to start.
9. When the unit beeps to show that it is preheated, open the lid.
10. Arrange the mozzarella sticks in "Air Fry Basket" and insert in the oven.
11. Serve warm

Nutrition: Calories 254 Fat 6.6 g Carbs 35.2 g Protein 12.8 g

Tortilla Chips

Basic Recipe

Preparation Time: 10 minutes

Cooking Time: 3 minutes

Servings: 3

Ingredients:

- 4 corn tortillas cut into triangles
- 1 tablespoon olive oil
- Salt, to taste

Directions:

1. Coat the tortilla chips with oi and then, sprinkle each side of the tortillas with salt.
2. Press "Power Button" of Air Fry Oven and turn the dial to select the "Air Fry" mode.
3. Press the Time button and again turn the dial to set the cooking time to 3 minutes.
4. Now push the Temp button and rotate the dial to set the temperature at 390 degrees F.
5. Press "Start/Pause" button to start.
6. When the unit beeps to show that it is preheated, open the lid.
7. Arrange the tortilla chips in "Air Fry Basket" and insert in the oven.

8. Serve warm.

Nutrition: Calories 110 Fat 5.6 g Carbs 14.3 g Protein 1.8 g

Apple Chips

Basic Recipe
Preparation Time: 10 minutes
Cooking Time: 8 minutes
Servings: 2

Ingredients:

- 1 apple, peeled, cored and thinly sliced
- 1 tablespoon sugar
- ½ teaspoon ground cinnamon
- Pinch of ground cardamom
- Pinch of ground ginger
- Pinch of salt

Directions:

1. In a bowl, add all the ingredients and toss to coat well.
2. Press "Power Button" of Air Fry Oven and turn the dial to select the "Air Fry" mode.
3. Press the Time button and again turn the dial to set the cooking time to 8 minutes
4. Now push the Temp button and rotate the dial to set the temperature at 390 degrees F.
5. Press "Start/Pause" button to start.
6. When the unit beeps to show that it is preheated, open the lid.

7. Arrange the apple chips in "Air Fry Basket" and insert in the oven.

Nutrition: Calories 83 Fat 0.2 g Carbs 22 g Protein 0.3 g

Kale Chips

Basic Recipe
Preparation Time: 10 minutes
Cooking Time: 3 minutes
Servings: 4

Ingredients:

- 1 head fresh kale, stems and ribs removed and cut into 1½ inch pieces
- 1 tablespoon olive oil
- 1 teaspoon soy sauce
- 1/8 teaspoon cayenne pepper
- Pinch of freshly ground black pepper

Directions:

1. In a large bowl and mix together all the ingredients.
2. Press "Power Button" of Air Fry Oven and turn the dial to select the "Air Fry" mode.
3. Press the Time button and again turn the dial to set the cooking time to 3 minutes
4. Now push the Temp button and rotate the dial to set the temperature at 390 degrees F.
5. Press "Start/Pause" button to start.
6. When the unit beeps to show that it is preheated, open the lid.

7. Arrange the apple chips in "Air Fry Basket" and insert in the oven.
8. Toss the kale chips once halfway through.

Nutrition: Calories 115 Fat 3.5 g 0.5 g Carbs 17.9 g Protein 5.2 g

Beet Chips

Basic Recipe
Preparation Time: 10 minutes
Cooking Time: 15 minutes
Servings: 6

Ingredients:

- 4 medium beetroots, peeled and thinly sliced
- 2 tablespoons olive oil
- ¼ teaspoon smoked paprika
- Salt, to taste

Directions:

1. In a large bowl and mix together all the ingredients.
2. Press "Power Button" of Air Fry Oven and turn the dial to select the "Air Fry" mode.
3. Press the Time button and again turn the dial to set the cooking time to 15 minutes
4. Now push the Temp button and rotate the dial to set the temperature at 325 degrees F.
5. Press "Start/Pause" button to start.
6. When the unit beeps to show that it is preheated, open the lid.
7. Arrange the apple chips in "Air Fry Basket" and insert in the oven.

8. Toss the beet chips once halfway through.
9. Serve at room temperature.

Nutrition: Calories 70 Fat 4.8 g Carbs 6.7 g Protein 1.1 g

Broccoli Salad with Goat Cheese

Basic Recipe
Preparation Time: 10 minutes
Cooking Time: 10 minutes
Servings: 4

Ingredients:

- 2 ounces broccoli florets
- 3 onions
- 3 and 1/2 ounces of goat cheese
- 4 tomatoes, sliced
- 4 bell peppers
- Cooking spray
- Salt and pepper, to taste

Directions:

1. Use cooking spray to coat bell peppers, broccoli, and onions
2. Preheat your air fry at 360 degrees F in "AIR FRY" mode
3. Cook for 10 minutes
4. Take a salad bowl and transfer the mixture into it
5. Add goat cheese and tomatoes on top
6. Then Season it with pepper and salt
7. Serve and enjoy!

Nutrition: Calories 380 Fat 15 g, Carbs 8 g, Protein 50g

Fried Pumpkin Seeds

Basic Recipe
Preparation Time: 10 minutes
Cooking Time: 50 minutes
Servings: 2

Ingredients:

- 1 and 1/2 cups pumpkin seeds
- Olive oil as needed
- 1 and 1/2 teaspoons salt
- 1 teaspoon smoked paprika

Directions:

1. Cut pumpkin and scrape out seeds and flesh
2. Separate flesh from seeds and rinse the seeds under cold water
3. Bring 2 quarter of salted water to boil and add seeds, boil for 10 minutes
4. Dry out seeds and spread them on a kitchen towel
5. Dry for 20 minutes
6. Preheat your fryer to 350 degrees F in "AIR FRY" mode
7. Take a bowl and add seeds, smoked paprika, and olive oil

8. Season it with salt and transfer to your Air Fryer cooking basket
9. Cook for 35 minutes, Enjoy!

Nutrition: Calories 270 Fat 21 g, Carbs 4 g, Protein 12g

Potato and Paprika Roast

Basic Recipe
Preparation Time: 35minutes
Cooking Time: 20 minutes
Servings: 4

Ingredients:

- 56 ounces potatoes, peeled and cubed
- 2 tablespoons spicy paprika
- 4 cups Greek yogurt
- 4 tablespoons olive oil, divided
- Salt and pepper, to taste

Directions:

1. Preheat your air fryer to 360 degrees F in "AIR FRY" mode
2. Soak the potatoes in water. Let it soak for 30 minutes. Take a paper towel then Dry out and pat dry

3. Add paprika, salt, pepper and half of oil in a bowl
4. Mix them well. Coat the potatoes in the mixture. Cook in the air fryer for 20 minutes
5. Meanwhile, blend the remaining oil and yogurt
6. Season it with salt and pepper
7. Serve with yogurt and enjoy!

Nutrition: Calories 540 Fat 15 g, Carbs 25gProtein 60g

Juicy Fish Nuggets

Basic Recipe

Preparation Time: 10 minutes

Cooking Time: 10 minutes

Servings: 4

Ingredients:

- 1-pound fresh cod
- 2 tablespoons olive oil
- 1/2 cup almond flour
- 2 large finely beaten eggs
- 1-2 cups almond meal
- Salt as needed

Directions:

1. Preheat your Air Fryer to 388 degrees F in "AIR FRY" mode
2. Take a food processor and add olive oil, almond meal, salt and blend
3. Take three bowls and add almond flour, almond meal, beaten eggs individually
4. Take costs and cut them into slices of 1-inch thickness and 2-inch length
5. Dredge slices into flour, eggs and in crumbs

6. Transfer nuggets to Air Fryer cooking basket and cook for 10 minutes until golden
7. Serve and enjoy!

Nutrition: Calories 200 Fat 14 g, Carbs 6 g, Protein 14g

Vegetable Cutlets

Basic Recipe
Preparation Time: 10 minutes
Cooking Time: 15 minutes
Servings: 6
Ingredients:

- 7 ounces potatoes
- 1/2 a carrot, grated
- 2 ounces capsicum, chopped
- 2 ounces cabbage, chopped
- Salt as needed
- Panko bread crumbs
- 1 teaspoons arrowroot mixed with water

Directions:

1. Take a pot of boiling water and add potatoes
2. Once the potatoes are boiled, take them out and let them cool

3. Peel the potatoes and mash them alongside cabbage, capsicum and season the mixture with salt
4. Divide the mixture into 6 balls
5. Flatten balls into cutlet shapes
6. Coat each ball with arrowroot slurry and dredge them in breadcrumbs
7. Pre-heat your Fryer to 356 degrees F in "AIR FRY" mode
8. Transfer balls to your Air Fryer cooking basket and cook for 8 minutes, give them a turn and cook for 8 minutes more
9. Serve and enjoy!

Nutrition: Calories 240 Fat 4 g Carbs 46 g Protein 7 g

Cumin and Squash Chili

Basic Recipe

Preparation Time: 10 minutes

Cooking Time: 16 minutes

Servings: 4

Ingredients:

- 1 medium butternut squash
- 2 teaspoons cumin seeds
- 1 large pinch chili flakes
- 1 tablespoon olive oil
- and 1/2-ounces pine nuts
- 1 small bunch fresh coriander, chopped

Directions:

1. Take the squash and slice it. Remove seeds and cut into smaller chunks
2. Take a bowl and add chunked squash, spice and oil
3. Mix well

4. Pre-heat your Fryer to 360 degrees F and add the squash to the cooking basket in "AIR FRY" mode
5. Roast for 20 minutes, making sure to shake the basket from time to time to avoid burning
6. Take a pan and place it over medium heat, add pine nuts to the pan and dry toast for 2 minutes
7. Sprinkle nuts on top of the squash and serve
8. Enjoy!

Nutrition: Calories 400 Fat 15 g Carbs 50 g Protein 16 g

Banana Fritters

Basic Recipe
Preparation Time: 10 minutes
Cooking Time: 16 minutes
Servings: 6

Ingredients:

- 1 medium butternut squash
- 2 teaspoons cumin seeds
- 1 large pinch chili flakes
- 1 tablespoon olive oil
- and 1/2-ounces pine nuts
- 1 small bunch fresh coriander, chopped

Directions:

1. Preheat your Air Fryer to 340 degrees F in "AIR FRY" mode
2. Take a bowl and add salt, sesame seeds, water and mix them well until a nice batter form
3. Coat the bananas with the flour mixture and transfer them to the fryer basket
4. Cook for 8 minutes
5. Enjoy!

Nutrition: Calories 240 Fat 10 g Carbs 30 g Protein 5 g

CONCLUSION

Air fryers are a relatively new piece of kitchen gadgetry. They are used by individuals who want to cook healthy foods using less oil and less fat then their conventional counterparts.

In addition to being a healthier alternative to deep frying, air fryers are also fun to use. Air-frying not only produces lots of fun and tasty food, it also saves you time and money. You can cook without the need of a griddle or a stovetop, which frees up your kitchen so you can focus on eating more healthy foods!

It is important to have an air fryer that is up to par. If you want an air fryer that will last for years, make sure that you buy an durable one. To help you choose the right air fryer for you, we have compiled a list of the best air fried ovens!

The Airfryer has several seating options. The four different versions include:

Small Seating–The size of the seating area is 13.5" x 8.5" x 9.5".

Medium Seating—The size of the seating area is 20" x 12".

Large Seating—The size of the seating area is 23" x 15".

Extra Large Seating—The size is 32" X 21". The extra large seat could accommodate up to 8 pieces. A small, medium or large fryer is included with every air fryer and can be purchased separately. The only part that may need to be purchased separately is a colander for the basket which will hold up to 16 cups depending on the size of the basket that you are using. There are no other accessories required for the air fryer: please see the specifications on this page for further details.

What's happening to our restaurant food? The answer is rather simple. We are over-cooking and over-frying foods, and most of it is for the wrong reasons.

Nobody wants to eat overcooked, undercooked, or under-salted food. Restaurant owners are turning away good customers in the name of profit.

That's not our fault. It's up to the professional chefs to do a better job with their cooking skills.

We use our Air Fryers to cook foods that don't require cooking at all. We use them to cook and heat our foods in such a way that they're ready to eat right out of the air fryer. There's no need for you to heat up your kitchen with a conventional oven or stove, just put the food in and let it finish fully. You'll be amazed at how delicious your foods can taste when you use an Air Fryer!

Today's busy lifestyle often leaves us with little time to cook. For those of you who don't have time to cook, but still need your food, the air fryer is for you.

An air fryer is an appliance that cooks food by circulating hot air over it. The circulating air causes the food to slowly cook within a sealed container while removing excess oil and fat from the food. By sealing the food in a hermetic chamber during cooking, no additional oil is released into the air. This is important because it prevents the flavor of the food from being compromised. The result is a fast and easy way to prepare delicious meals without having to use any grease or oils while eroding your pantry of oils.

In this air fryer cookbook, we will teach you how to use your air fryer most effectively and how to avoid common mistakes. From learning how to clean and maintain your air fryer to finding creative recipes, this guide will help you get the most out of your air fryer today